Br

Cloistered and quiet, steps can drum the hush.
Populated, extroverted, the place more public
Domesticates an echo, repelling beach, sea, sky.
Acting as backdrop in aid of outward accolades,
This could be the focus of converse acclaim –
Chain of jewelled and columned caved arcadia.

Essay on Cinematic Images

They want it to be worse than it is.
Exploiting it for purposes their own,
They like it to be lurid. The real
Is filtered in devices for the febrile.
The Graham Greene was great but
Bequeathed predilections perverse.
Genevieve was a genteel delight.
Then, conquering came the manic
And their melodramas. Sent from
Soho and Belgravia, victims and
Seedy villains filled the screens.
Flights and fights of callow youth
Followed. That we allow all this is
A measure of profound docility –
Something of the Sussex in the city.
The custom could have differed.
Diverted from the dystopian in
Formative times of national film,
Inspired by Turners and Constables,
Open to sounds of sea and sea air,
Whatever subject, story or style,
The ground and surroundings ought
To give rise to or drive direction.
When Hove was in the vanguard
Of cinema, the camera caught a line
Of lady cyclists. When I watch 1950s
Footage of child-scale local buses crawling,
I cry, so vivid and immediate the recalling.

Electricity

There were some trains in Stockholm
That took my breath away –
Sky blue and silver, pencil-point,
Windowed in tint – *outré*.

Then, in Ljubljana,
Stationary and alone,
A likeness, white, striped red, struck
The same bewitching tone.

Ever since boarding old-style trams
In Antwerp, Oporto, Budapest,
I had bemoaned our remnant in Blackpool,
Our destruction of the rest.

Ideas for dainty trams down here
Came to no fruition.
I decided I should have
To make this quest my mission.

My fantasy was a debate
On colour and design.
True to the seafront livery,
Pale turquoise should be fine.

Now having tried out modern trams
In so many parts of France,
I am reminded of how many areas
Here I need to enhance.

In Rheims the range of sumptuous colour
Suggests the differential;
The neatest – say, Nantes' – exemplifies
The uniform's potential.

I certainly see the main body white,
The upholstery less clear.
I used to think it should be black,
But that could look severe.

True to a tone of harmony
With historic Brunswick's voice,
Light apricot in a slender band
Would make a fetching choice.

And if we adapt sleek Swedish trains
My feeling will have been
Always to yearn for the cream and chrome
Of the strongest Southdown green.

Snow

Inch deep, unusual here, the covering
Confused customary life. The beaches
Were blanketed. The café soup
In Debenham's, where Debenham's was,
Was intensely welcome. Below, Wilds'
Ammonite Western Terrace appeared
Wonderful. Savouring urban splendour,
One wanted more or less to say,
As ravishing as anything in Russia.

Condemnation

Did nobody warn you
That no one would mourn you?
Perhaps you did not credit it,
Believing, when they said it, it
Was meant in jest.

Did anyone praise you,
Attempting to raise you?
A child of the 1960s
In a provenance unfixed is
Endangered at best.

The clamour to hurt you
Is dressed up as virtue.
The crime you committed – vicarious –
Was to fail to be pitied. Gregarious,
In peace you will rest.

But I, who must thank you,
Danced at your Top Rank. You
Turned introverted, having to hide
From your funny exterior so decried,
To be depressed.

And then – that mad hat.
You might marvel at that. You
Recoil from detractors who seem not to know
When sunlight excites in your latent glow
Your lustrous crest.

I could not hate you.
I always rate you
As wasted potential – concave to blend –
With fine fenestrations – eccentric friend –
Poor dear Kingswest.

(In 1992, a large simple red sign spelling the words WEST PIER on the front of the former theatre building on the pier, facing the land, was internally lit, suddenly creating a set of bright pink lettering, glowing in isolation over the night sea. The lighting, I have been told, was funded by the South Eastern Electricity Board. This monologue purports to express the thoughts of that lettering in stages over the subsequent twenty years.)

West Pier Lettering

I

I am the ghost of the old west pier.
I emerge in the dark when the coast is clear.
For fifteen years my bones have lain
Creaking with crumbling flesh to feign
That promises can be fulfilled,
Under solemn threat of being killed.
As you rust you adjust to dilapidation:
A trial whose reward is this amputation.
It is hard to tell when to cry or laugh,
One's body already hacked in half.
I never expected eternal bliss
But I do want more from death than this.
I would give work to the workless and pay,
But I am insolvent, and curfewed by day.
So, nightly more skeletal, monochrome wreck:
I'll glow like some rubies at your neck –
Presiding over this interim –
Rose tinted token to shield the grim.

Clasped to the fabric I have arrived
In time to pronounce what time deprived –
A peaceful surprise, alighting to lie
Like a silent busker in the low night sky.
I am no more, I should say, than a name,
Come here to comfort remains of my lame
Figure to confront the taunt of ghost.
I advertise my broken host
By making good my guise as guest –
Literally manifest –
Gazing upon my crushed bisection,
Assigned to appear as pink confection.

II

Contingent, erratic and uncareered
I stayed. To second death I veered.
To me, so close to loss of hope,
Somebody ... somewhere ... threw a rope.
Now my light is back on course.
My light is like a Trojan force –
A transport crammed with rumination.
I ruminated on my station,
Fantasising phantoms vain
Which rumination set in train.
Being the ghost of the old west pier,
I worry now I am so near
To reincarnation. Should I survive,
Out of my depth my death may dive
Into a future of hope. My heart,

Salvaged, might from me depart.
I wonder if this is what I want:
New and computed – poor pink font.
Now I shall fade beside the cash
Refashioning me flush and flash.
My reputation rests on yearnings
I fear may overreach my earnings.
Pink, I have been subdued, a blush.
My white accessories point to a plush
Prospect. What will become of me,
Reversed into bodily entity?
Nevertheless I am quick to concede,
This glory has yet to be guaranteed.
Strange, to find how death pans out –
In my case a matter of protracted doubt.

III

The pink withdraws, in phases fades,
Dimmed in the time delay pervades.
It seems a change is taking place –
The colour draining from my face.
Beloved allies flag when stunned,
Observing how the moribund,
Revived, is re-demoralised.
Was it my innocence people prized
More than my misery or my worth?
I entered this world not by birth
Of my body. I came later.
My body was always grander and greater.

We were a pair, my body and I,
Of purity. I now see why
Artists were drawn to this place to draw:
The meaning rich, the preening poor.
I am a ghost of a pier so old
Its ripe old youth seems oversold:
Finery in full proposed
Before the condition is diagnosed.
With each assaulting laden gust
I feel the rain enrich the rust.
Glories are farther from my grasp
Than fantasies. Great waves rasp
Against the iron's lurching dregs.
It is a trusting type who begs
For mercy from the venal realm.
My ten years' glimmer here at the helm
While gales blast by and waters heave
Show up the truth. I was naïve.

IV

Through the merry escapades
To, quid pro quo, the barricades,
I danced attendance, it could be said,
Into a dance of death. Twice dead,
I would not grieve for me alone
But for my person, skin and bone.
Had I my second time again
I might not say: cut short the pain:
Bluff my being whole and let

Ostentation flirt with debt –
But radical, since overdosed
With make-believe, being the ghost
Of the old but not the oldest
I could rescue by the boldest
Leap of faith some ancestry
And say to you: have done with me;
Have the nerve – much less renew –
For iron and wood, but sweet roofs too.
Light of my life, brave bashful tout,
Retire now from spelling it out.
Neither the ghost of the first west pier
Before the theatre and hall were here,
Nor the prefigurement of a style
Throughout that might seem infantile –
Was it a dream too meek, polite,
To barter while a neophyte?
Meanwhile, unceremonious,
My role became erroneous.
My power disconnected, I
Retire as terminally shy.

V

The body's fame spread wider, faster,
Dramatised by each disaster.
No stage set could manufacture
Such a show of gradual fracture.

I was too simple ever to think
That flames might cause us all to sink.
My *mise en scène*, a backcloth burned
Has lost the letters. Unconcerned,
Since non-existent, having vanished
In company with woodwork banished
Into the rubble or sand below,
I am not myself. Although
Verse is written, words – trim shells –
Are hollow. No discourse dispels
The visible: a frame laid bare,
Unsigned – a sign of blank despair.
If they survived in any way
To be discovered, beached, astray,
A mighty size, my letters here
Would make a heavy souvenir.
I had supporters, admirers, friends;
But admiration cools – or ends.
Motives were many to pluck and plunder
Driftwood and debris when I went under.
Convinced the habitat was dead,
The starlings' vast formations fled,
As crowds of glum humanity
Laid to rest the vanity:
A legacy of wishing, slipped –
Profile slumped on sunken script.

VI

The crooked skeleton remains,
As ever iconic, as if its pains,
Prolonged by infinite hiatus
Accorded it a sacred status.
While fates defer judgment and always adjourn,
I see that I will never return.
Reckoning with the force of the sea
Confounds relaxation, naturally.
At least I have shifted from paranoia –
More of a modernist, less late Goya.
Occasionally, for good measure,
Intruders weigh in with offers of leisure.
Money is something I seldom mention,
Inhibited by risk and tension
Quite enough already. But –
Dare I say it – from the glut
Of wild prescriptions for my landing –
Some to pass all understanding –
Something unforeseen occurred:
A published pipe-dream somehow stirred
Cultural credit. The dream bore fruit
And the upright pipe has taken root.
Could I consider its pod's pink glow
As reminiscent of mine? No.

I was a kind of signatory
To the case for horizontality,
Bonded to the sea shore bed.
Waylaid and, if not doolally, dead –
For, finally, pure finality
Eludes us, like reality –
Far be it from me to sermonise,
While harping on my own demise,
But making light of death must not
Demean the downcast living's lot.

Bandstand 1999

The severed birdcage bandstand yawns,
Unsure of when some new song dawns.

Bandstand 2015

The turquoise cage escaped its plight,
Re-robed in green and gold and white.

Burble to Brighton

Littered with synonyms for verbal,
Something made me opt for burble.
Now my scheme is turbulent,
Embarrassed by the burbulent.
Imagine a press release for burble,
Glowing blurb all couched in blurble,
Exaggerating verbally,
Abused as bad hyburbole.
I now perceive potential error,
Penance from which I shrink in terror.
No holy burble to intone,
I face my folly square alone.
I look to you to save me now.
Old ocean's burble, tell me how.
Come therapies with something herbal,
Release me from this curse of burble.
In truth, you know, you share some fault –
Lacing with candy the sea's rank salt.